The Winston Grammar Program

BASIC LEVEL
Student's Workbook

Paul R. Erwin

The contents of this book are fully protected under the copyright and patent laws of the United States. No part of this book may be reproduced without the express written consent of the author.

© COPYRIGHT 1992

Precious Memories Educational Resources
18403 NE 111th Ave.
Battleground, WA 98604
(360) 687-0282

ISBN: 1-889673-00-5 (Complete Set)
ISBN: 1-889673-01-3 (Student Package)
ISBN: 1-889673-03-X (Student Workbook)

Copyright© 1992. Reprinted 2006 by Precious Memories Educational Resources. All rights reserved. No part of this publication may be reproduced, stored in a retrieval system, or transmitted in any form or by any means, without prior written permission of Precious Memories Educational Resources.
Printed in the United States of America.

The contents of *The Winston Grammar Program* are fully protected under the patent laws of the United States.

Contents

In *The Winston Grammar Program* learning is incremental, with each lesson building upon previously-learned material. All lessons after the first, therefore, contain some built-in review. Most lessons introduce a new concept stated as a focus in the following list; however, some lessons are entirely review work.

WORKSHEET	FOCUS
1	Articles and Nouns
2	Common and Proper Nouns
3	Review
4	Personal Pronouns
5	Review
6	Verbs
7	Review
8	Helping Verbs
9	Contractions
10	Interrogative Sentences
11	Adjectives
12	Adverbs
13	Review
14	Modification
15	Prepositions
16	Prepositional Phrases
17	Review
18	Coordinating Conjunctions
19	Review
20	Interjections
21	Review
22	The Ellipsis
23	Subjects
24	Action and Linking Verbs
25	Direct Objects
26	Indirect Objects
27	Predicate Nominatives
28	Review
29	Nouns of Direct Address
30	Appositives

Pretest

Write your answers to the following questions on the lines at the right.

Sentence 1

The old truck chugged slowly along the highway.

1. Name the adjective. _____ 1.
2. Name the adverb. _____ 2.
3. Name the preposition. _____ 3.
4. Name the subject. _____ 4.
5. Name the object of the preposition. _____ 5.
6. What word does *slowly* modify? _____ 6.

Sentence 2

She gave Dan a nice gift yesterday.

7. Name the direct object. _____ 7.
8. Name the adverb. _____ 8.
9. Name the verb. _____ 9.
10. Name the pronoun. _____ 10.
11. Name the article. _____ 11.
12. Name the indirect object. _____ 12.
13. What word does *nice* modify? _____ 13.

Copyright © 1992, 1982
Permission is granted to reproduce this test for use with *The Winston Grammar Program*.

Sentence 3

Do not take a nap before dinner, Teddy.

14. How many nouns are there in Sentence 3? _____ 14.

15. Name the direct object. _____ 15.

16. Name the noun of direct address. _____ 16.

17. Name the subject. _____ 17.

18. Name the verb phrase. _____ 18.

19. Name the adverb. _____ 19.

Sentence 4

They are ready for the game, and I hope they will win.

20. Name the coordinating conjunction. _____ 20.

21. Name the helping verb. _____ 21.

22. Name the "being" or "linking" verb. _____ 22.

23. How many subjects are there in Sentence 4? _____ 23.

24. Name the adjective. _____ 24.

Sentence 5

Ouch, the stove is very hot!

25. Name the verb. _____ 25.

26. Name the adverb. _____ 26.

27. Name the interjection. _____ 27.

28. Name the article. _____ 28.

Sentence 6

Donna and I are the new captains of the golf team.

29. How many adjectives are there in Sentence 6? _____ 29.

30. Name the object of the preposition. _____ 30.

31. Name the subject(s). _____ 31.

32. Name the predicate nominative. _____ 32.

33. What part of speech is *golf*? _____ 33.

WORKSHEET 1

- Put a check (√) over the articles.
- Underline the nouns once.

1. The button on the doorbell rings in the house.

2. We opened an old chest in the attic.

3. She took a plane to the college.

4. The man took the kitten into the house.

5. A girl in the class quickly found the hamster.

6. The doctor left an umbrella on the table.

7. He called a plumber; the drainpipe was very clogged.

8. Yesterday the best team won the big game.

9. The variety show was very good.

10. The monster in the movie frightened me.

11. The farmer raises cows and horses.

12. The team was happy with the new coach.

WORKSHEET

- Put a check (√) over articles.
- Underline all common and proper nouns once.
- Remember that proper nouns made of more than one word are underlined with one continous line.

1. Jacob moved from Detroit to San Diego.

2. Nettie DeSisto was a fan of Elvis Presley.

3. Ms. Brady is a good citizen.

4. We have an idea for the game.

5. I saw Ms. Frye at the grocery store today.

6. Bernard Roth and Sally Mason went to the opera.

7. We saw seals and whales at Marineland in Florida.

8. Carol Frost is a pilot for Trans World Airlines.

9. The United States is close to Canada on the map.

10. The Dallas Cowboys won the Super Bowl.

11. The real name for the dog is Clyde.

12. They watched *Gone with the Wind* on television.

WORKSHEET 3

- Put a check (√) over articles.
- Underline nouns once.

1. The governor signed the bill after the debate.

2. He raises roses and tulips in the backyard.

3. During the summer, Wesley and Megan go to an overnight camp.

4. Bob Hope gave a show for the soldiers in Saudi Arabia.

5. Be careful; we have seen bears in the park.

6. We saw no troopers on the road near the accident.

7. She went to medical school at Harvard University.

8. Colorado and Wyoming are west of St. Louis.

9. The tools in the shed were returned to Mr. Nasser.

10. They attended a party on New Year's Eve.

11. Don Martin arrived on a crowded bus.

12. Uncle Karl took me to a game at Bass River Park.

WORKSHEET 4

- Put a check (√) over articles.
- Underline nouns once.
- Write *pron.* over personal pronouns.

1. Shall I tell them about the party?

2. Florida is pleasant during the winter, Leo.

3. A brave hiker climbed Mt. Washington.

4. On February 5th, they will meet us in Chicago.

5. He and the boss make important decisions together.

6. World War II was over by 1946.

7. You will see her in school tomorrow.

8. Worms in the garden make the soil healthy.

9. They went to St. Luke's Hospital during visiting hours.

10. She would enjoy an afternoon at a museum.

11. On Independence Day, we celebrate the birth of the country.

WORKSHEET 5

- Put a check (√) over articles.
- Underline nouns once.
- Write *pron.* over personal pronouns.

1. The knights returned from the royal tournament.

2. During the day, owls and bats sleep in the trees.

3. She and I slowly climbed the hill on bicycles.

4. The championship game was played on a muddy field.

5. He and I are officers in the Lions Club.

6. Ms. Batal, a lawyer, came to the house today.

7. Johnny, will you please pass us the cake?

8. Early in the twentieth century, people did not have radios.

9. They will go to the game tomorrow with Aunt Louise.

10. San Francisco is on the coast of the Pacific Ocean.

11. The election is not over, but we know the results.

12. Marcia presented an award to him at the banquet.

WORKSHEET 6

- In each blank, fill in the correct form of the verb.

1. I will _kick_____
   Yesterday I _____
   I have _____

2. I will _see_____
   Yesterday I _____
   I have _____

3. I will _____
   Yesterday I _spoke_____
   I have _____

4. I will _____
   Yesterday I _ate_____
   I have _____

5. I will _____
   Yesterday I _____
   I have _written_____

6. I will _____
   Yesterday I _____
   I have _opened_____

- Put a check (√) over articles.
- Underline nouns once.
- Write *pron.* over personal pronouns.
- Underline verbs twice.

1. We ate fruit and nuts after dinner.

2. The new mayor was a speaker at the parade.

3. The engineer jumped from the train carefully.

4. Mr. Sonbolian greeted her at the door.

5. She swims twenty laps in the pool before breakfast.

WORKSHEET 7

- Put a check (√) over articles.
- Underline nouns once.
- Write *pron.* over personal pronouns.
- Underline verbs twice.

1. Florence Nightingale helped many soldiers in the Crimean War.

2. I wanted a good performance yesterday.

3. The young teacher collects stamps and coins.

4. A tall gentleman stood in the doorway.

5. We worked hard in class today.

6. Flash caught a mouse in the cellar.

7. Before a storm, the air is heavy and still.

8. Seth Dator writes poems, and I write stories.

9. Early in the twentieth century, children worked in factories.

10. A firefighter helped the child down the ladder.

11. The tired swimmers rested on the beach.

12. Olivia held the stopwatch during the race.

QUIZ 1

(to be taken after completing Worksheet 7)

- Put a check (√) over articles.
- Underline all common and proper nouns once.
- Write *pron.* over personal pronouns.
- Underline verbs twice.

1. An honest person deserves respect from us.

2. He and I enjoyed a fancy meal.

3. In some countries, the government controls what people read.

4. *Little Women* is a favorite book of many children.

5. Henry Williams and Peter Hawkins fought for the Union in the Civil War.

6. A pot of soup simmered on the stove.

7. We found an unusual seashell at the beach.

8. Helen Keller was blind and deaf, but she overcame these handicaps.

9. South Junior High and Parker are the new schools in town.

10. On July 4th, they always go to the country for a picnic.

Bonus

In 1964, Martin Luther King, Jr. received the Nobel Prize for peace.

WORKSHEET 8

- Put a check (√) over articles.
- Underline nouns once.
- Write *pron.* over personal pronouns.
- Underline verbs twice.
- Watch for helping verbs.

1. I have gone to the movies already today.

2. The White Sox might be in the playoffs now.

3. You will find the papers on the desk.

4. All students should be polite in class.

5. The giraffes had eaten the leaves from the tops of the trees.

6. The heavy rains kept the farmers from the fields.

7. I may try some of the new games tomorrow.

8. A student can write a report in the library.

9. The company might move to New York.

10. I do not enjoy horror movies.

11. The baby could speak very clearly.

12. The mittens were knitted by Grandmother.

WORKSHEET 9

- Put a check (√) over articles.
- Underline nouns once.
- Write *pron.* over personal pronouns.
- Underline verbs twice.
- Watch for contractions.

1. She's not afraid of snakes or mice.

2. We'll miss them over the weekend.

3. I'll stay here during the parade.

4. We've counted the pennies in the jar.

5. He'll read the first story in the book.

6. They'd like the pizza better with peppers on it.

7. You're the best dog in the show, Sam.

8. I've never been to Japan or China.

9. We'd enjoy a trip to South America.

10. I'm sure it's correct.

11. They're in college, but I'm not.

12. You'll hide behind the tree.

WORKSHEET 10

- Identify all parts of speech that have been learned so far.
- Watch for interrogative sentences.

1. Is Detroit located near the Great Lakes?

2. They'll be late for the party, and I'll be angry.

3. Robin Hood stole from rich people and helped poor people.

4. Can you be in Denver on January 8, 1994?

5. I thought you'd give her a chance.

6. Do the peanuts make you thirsty?

7. The little children enjoyed the clowns at the circus.

8. Did Tanya go into the store for a newspaper?

9. The boy smiled at the new puppy.

10. She's been in Africa with the Peace Corps.

11. The president lives in the White House in Washington, D.C.

12. Will the old riverboat ever carry passengers again?

WORKSHEET 11

- Identify all parts of speech learned so far.
- Remember to write *adj.* over adjectives.

1. The young pony is cute and frisky.

2. We'll have hot rolls and eggs today.

3. The deep cut on the arm has healed.

4. On winter mornings, the old car always starts.

5. Ramona spilled green paint on the kitchen floor.

6. A thin layer of dust covered the floor.

7. The sharp drill will go through the wood.

8. He loved the beautiful beaches in Puerto Rico.

9. Stormy weather sells umbrellas at the department store.

10. The meal was delicious at the Log Cabin Inn.

11. The cold water refreshed the thirsty bikers.

12. I'll look for the red bottle on the back shelf.

WORKSHEET

- Identify all parts of speech learned so far.
- Remember to write *adj.* over adjectives and *adv.* over adverbs.

1. The bullfrog quickly hopped across the muddy bank.

2. The fields are pretty in the French painting.

3. Today we had a picnic under the elm tree.

4. We're happy about the new puppy.

5. Business will slowly improve later in the year.

6. Will you stay and have a snack with us?

7. We've been on the trail for three days.

8. The rubber band wrapped the papers tightly.

9. South America isn't cold near the Equator.

10. I recently read *To Kill a Mockingbird*.

11. The pencil is dull; I'll sharpen it.

12. Never dive into shallow water, Betsy.

13. An old necklace was found here yesterday.

WORKSHEET 13

- Identify all parts of speech learned so far.

1. The carpenter carefully cut the lumber for the cabinets.

2. I'll always buy groceries on the weekends.

3. A shiny red apple appeared on the desk today.

4. Elephants aren't often found in European zoos.

5. First, you connect the wires to the small battery.

6. The students were good listeners, and they asked a few questions.

7. You returned from the hardware store quickly.

8. We should divide the cards into equal piles.

9. Tomorrow she'll take a bus to Miami Beach.

10. Can you see it now, Ms. Johnson?

11. Marcus couldn't decide on a name for the kitten.

12. Henri put the hammer and nails neatly on the workbench.

13. You might leave the dog outside.

QUIZ

(to be taken after completing Worksheet 13)

- Put a check (√) over articles.
- Underline nouns once.
- Write *pron.* over personal pronouns.
- Underline verbs twice.
- Write *adj.* over adjectives.
- Write *adv.* over adverbs.

1. I'm not in the chess club, Ms. Bergeron.

2. In the general store, you can buy candy for a penny.

3. It often snows heavily during the winter months in the Midwest.

4. Isn't Butch a builder in New Orleans?

5. She had taped the important message securely on the refrigerator door.

6. Tomorrow they'll learn the correct bus route.

7. Could we have the surprise party here?

8. She drew a large circle around it with chalk.

9. Immediately we became suspicious.

10. He might be happy now.

Bonus

Won't you ever go outside?

WORKSHEET

- Identify all parts of speech learned so far.
- Draw arrows from adjectives and adverbs to the words they modify.

1. Pure water is delicious on a hot day.

2. Baseball wasn't always popular in Japan.

3. The bright torch lit the cave very nicely.

4. Aunt Dolores phoned and told us about the blizzard in New England.

5. Tiny snakes are sometimes quite dangerous.

6. We will plant an oak tree there.

7. The spaceship landed safely on the back side of the moon.

8. I won't go too far into the dense jungle.

9. Always close the windows during a thunderstorm.

10. The ugly fish suddenly frightened the brave diver.

11. The plumber can't fix the leaky sink today.

12. Luckily, I found the coins on the rug.

WORKSHEET 15

- Identify all parts of speech learned so far.
- Draw arrows from adjectives and adverbs to the words they modify.
- Remember to write *prep.* over a preposition and put a (in front of a preposition.

1. We hid the presents under the bed.

2. They played outside near the pond yesterday.

3. Aren't you hungry in the morning?

4. They dug for clams on the sandbar at low tide.

5. You may go into the house for a drink.

6. In Australia, it's winter in August.

7. Celia often rides to school with Ms. Pope.

8. You shouldn't talk too loudly during the movie.

9. She'll be at the race on Saturday.

10. I was sick on the day of the festival.

11. She laughed at the silly joke in the paper.

12. Roberto will take a bus to Mexico City today.

WORKSHEET 16

- Identify all parts of speech learned so far.
- Draw arrows from adjectives and adverbs to the words they modify.
- Write *O.P.* over the object of a preposition.
- Enclose prepositional phrases within parentheses.
- Label each prepositional phrase with either *ADJ.* or *ADV.*
- Draw arrows from prepositional phrases to the words they modify.

1. The heavy traffic moved slowly through the tunnel.

2. Vic served in the Army for several years.

3. Very shiny objects will attract fish to the net.

4. In ancient Rome, men fought with lions at the Colosseum.

5. The laborer couldn't work for several weeks.

6. She played an electric guitar in the concert.

7. Harlem is a section of Manhattan.

8. Great literature and music have been created in Harlem.

9. I left the new store after Jim Owens.

10. The children sold lemonade under the trees by the roadside.

11. Before class, the teacher collected the papers.

12. Ms. Zebroski wasn't present at the wedding yesterday.

13. The vendor on the sidewalk is selling bags of peanuts.

WORKSHEET

- Identify all parts of speech learned so far.
- Draw arrows from adjectives and adverbs to the words they modify.
- Write *O.P.* over the object of a preposition.
- Enclose prepositional phrases within parentheses.
- Label each prepositional phrase with either *ADJ.* or *ADV.*
- Draw arrows from prepositional phrases to the words they modify.

1. Beyond the hill, we found a beautiful little pond.

2. Fido quickly ran and hid under the porch.

3. I don't like milk in coffee.

4. She knows the guest from Lebanon.

5. She bought a new car at the local dealership.

6. We have big problems with the new highway.

7. A long letter from Mr. Chung arrived today.

8. The barber doesn't cut hair for children.

9. The dirty air in the mines is dangerous.

10. Stir the soup on the stove, Larry.

11. Three members of the tribe came to the camp in a canoe.

12. Poor safety habits cause accidents on the road.

WORKSHEET 18

- Identify all parts of speech learned so far.
- Remember to write *c.c.* over coordinating conjunctions.
- Draw arrows from adjectives and adverbs to the words they modify.
- Write *O.P.* over the object of a preposition.
- Enclose prepositional phrases within parentheses.
- Label each prepositional phrase with either *ADJ.* or *ADV.*
- Draw arrows from prepositional phrases to the words they modify.

1. She's very confident, but he's nervous.

2. It was cold and windy on the shore of Lake Huron.

3. The machine in the shop was old yet useful.

4. The mysterious woman left, but she'll return soon.

5. The library is down the street and around the corner.

6. Armando is very happy, for he will go to Acapulco tomorrow.

7. I will invite Anna or Rosalie to the race at the club.

8. The Marine Corps and the Navy have new uniforms.

9. Were you at home or in school yesterday?

10. The pencils and pens haven't arrived yet.

11. We'll visit the museums and art galleries in Los Angeles.

12. They must improve, or they'll never win.

WORKSHEET

- Identify all parts of speech learned so far.
- Draw arrows from adjectives and adverbs to the words they modify.
- Write O.P. over the object of a preposition.
- Enclose prepositional phrases within parentheses.
- Label each prepositional phrase with either *ADJ.* or *ADV.*
- Draw arrows from prepositional phrases to the words they modify.

1. I want a new car, but I can't afford it.

2. Will you go with us or stay with her?

3. The operation was a success; he'll be healthy soon.

4. The rabbit ran across the field and into the woods.

5. Fumiko bought bread, jam, and cookies for lunch.

6. In a few minutes, you'll learn the answer.

7. Maria studied hard, and she passed the test.

8. She found three books, but she couldn't choose among them.

9. The lion cubs lay in the sun near the edge of the river.

10. The steel workers asked the boss a question.

11. Recently, many people from Cambodia have arrived in the United States.

12. We made too much noise and frightened the birds away.

WORKSHEET 20

- Identify all parts of speech learned so far.
- Remember to write ! over interjections.
- Draw arrows from adjectives and adverbs to the words they modify.
- Write *O.P.* over the object of a preposition.
- Enclose prepositional phrases within parentheses.
- Label each prepositional phrase with either *ADJ.* or *ADV.*
- Draw arrows from prepositional phrases to the words they modify.

1. Hey, didn't you see me?

2. We would have gone, but we were busy.

3. Help me, Tina; I need some information.

4. Yuck! I hate stale cookies.

5. The teenagers loved the loud music on the radio.

6. The old car made funny noises.

7. Ah, now I understand the problem!

8. Wow! Look at the monkey in the tree.

9. Yea! The turkey will be ready soon.

10. Whoops! I slipped on the ice.

11. May we have silence in the room?

12. Oh, I didn't know about the rule against shorts in school.

WORKSHEET

- Identify all parts of speech learned so far.
- Draw arrows from adjectives and adverbs to the words they modify.
- Write O.P. over the object of a preposition.
- Enclose prepositional phrases within parentheses.
- Label each prepositional phrase with either *ADJ.* or *ADV.*
- Draw arrows from prepositional phrases to the words they modify.

1. It is much colder in Moscow today.

2. The coach gave the football team a fiery pep talk before the game.

3. Frost damaged the vegetables in the garden.

4. Oh, I didn't know the answer.

5. I'll read the long report to her.

6. She could see a doctor about the injury.

7. Read the directions and start the motor.

8. The happy boy lighted the candles on the cake.

9. A policewoman gave Carmen a ticket yesterday in Mayberry.

10. The small child tossed the ball into the air.

11. After one lesson, Vito could ski beautifully.

12. You can connect the dots on the paper.

QUIZ 3

(to be taken after completing Worksheet 21)

- Identify all parts of speech learned so far.
- Draw arrows from adjectives and adverbs to the words they modify.
- Write *O.P.* over the object of a preposition.
- Enclose prepositional phrases within parentheses.
- Label each prepositional phrase with either *ADJ.* or *ADV.*
- Draw arrows from prepositional phrases to the words they modify.

1. Amy and Erin won't be at home today.

2. I have never been to Wyoming, but I am going there soon.

3. Oh, the summer is passing too quickly!

4. A wise person eats the right food and gets enough exercise.

5. During the storm, we stood in the doorway of the building.

6. Good strawberries aren't always available.

7. At the end of the pep rally, the new cheerleader was very hoarse.

8. Do you know the rules of the game, or shall I tell them to you?

9. At the Olympics, Olga Korbut did a backwards somersault on the parallel bars.

10. Close the back door before dinner, Marcello.

Bonus

Gee, I'm already rather old for the team.

WORKSHEET

- Identify all parts of speech learned so far.
- Don't forget that some pronouns may be omitted. When this is the case, write in the pronoun and enclose it within parentheses.
- Draw arrows from adjectives and adverbs to the words they modify.
- Write *O.P.* over the object of a preposition.
- Enclose prepositional phrases within parentheses.
- Label each prepositional phrase with either *ADJ.* or *ADV.*
- Draw arrows from prepositional phrases to the words they modify.

1. Empty the garbage now.

2. Hurry home after the game, Felicia.

3. Thank you again for the ride to the dance.

4. Do you need the tools and the ladder?

5. Hey! Leave the pool immediately.

6. On January 1st, we will go to the Cotton Bowl.

7. Write a friendly note to the director.

8. Carry the books with both hands.

9. Are you happy about the grade you received in biology?

10. Check the mail and pay the bills.

11. Look for rare birds on the trip through the jungle.

12. Don't forget the tape; we'll play it at the party.

WORKSHEET 23

- Identify all parts of speech learned so far.
- Draw arrows from adjectives and adverbs to the words they modify.
- Write *O.P.* over the object of a preposition.
- Enclose prepositional phrases within parentheses.
- Label each prepositional phrase with either *ADJ.* or *ADV.*
- Draw arrows from prepositional phrases to the words they modify.
- Use Noun Function Card 1; put an *S.* over each subject.

1. Mother rides a bus to the office.

2. We had a flat tire on the busy highway.

3. Is he in the office today, Ms. Najinsky?

4. Mr. Goldberg took the baseball team to Yankee Stadium for the game with the Detroit Tigers.

5. The door won't open; I can't get outside.

6. The big, shaggy collie produced ten pups.

7. George Washington Carver found many uses for peanut shells.

8. Grandmother volunteers at the new community hospital.

9. Riverboat rides don't make me ill.

10. After the boat trip, we will walk to the center of town.

11. Dr. Wu is an excellent dentist.

12. She and I won't arrive until Sunday.

WORKSHEET 24

- Identify all parts of speech learned so far.
- Draw arrows from adjectives and adverbs to the words they modify.
- Write *O.P.* over the object of a preposition.
- Enclose prepositional phrases within parentheses.
- Label each prepositional phrase with either *ADJ.* or *ADV.*
- Draw arrows from prepositional phrases to the words they modify.
- Use Noun Function Card 1; put an *S.* over each subject.
- Use Noun Function Card 2; tell whether the main verb is action or linking by circling the correct letter at the end of each sentence.

1. The rodeo clown jumped into the barrel.   A L

2. She is on the class list.   A L

3. On Saturdays, we eat dinner at different restaurants.   A L

4. You seem sad today.   A L

5. The ugly duckling became a swan.   A L

6. You should be happy about the final score.   A   L

7. She drinks coffee early in the morning.   A   L

8. The story couldn't be true.   A   L

9. The office will be built before the end

   of the year.   A   L

10. The old firetruck was bright and shiny.   A   L

WORKSHEET 25

- Identify all parts of speech learned so far.
- If a pronoun has been omitted, write it in and enclose it within parentheses.
- Draw arrows from adjectives and adverbs to the words they modify.
- Write *O.P.* over the object of a preposition.
- Enclose prepositional phrases within parentheses.
- Label each prepositional phrase with either *ADJ.* or *ADV.*
- Draw arrows from prepositional phrases to the words they modify.
- Use Noun Function Cards 1–3:
    Put an *S.* over each subject.
    Circle each direct object.

1. Bernie fed two rabbits yesterday.

2. Ms. Grillo will be on the airplane today.

3. Uncle Eli painted the big picture over the fireplace.

4. She learned the alphabet in kindergarten.

5. We made fudge and brownies for the children.

6. She walked down the cellar stairs.

7. Naomi is patient, but Elysia isn't.

8. Mr. Frisbee came to the meeting early tonight.

9. We found many shells at the seashore.

10. Get the shovel, the rake, and the broom from the shed.

WORKSHEET 26

- Identify all parts of speech learned so far.
- Draw arrows from adjectives and adverbs to the words they modify.
- Write *O.P.* over the object of a preposition.
- Enclose prepositional phrases within parentheses.
- Label each prepositional phrase with either *ADJ.* or *ADV.*
- Draw arrows from prepositional phrases to the words they modify.
- Use Noun Function Cards 1–4:
    Put an *S.* over each subject.
    Circle each direct object.
    Put a box around each indirect object.

1. Ms. Mitsakos gave Owen a good book in English class.

2. I threw the ball to Claude.

3. Harry and I sent Natasha and Yuri a wedding gift.

4. The detective showed us the footprints in the snow.

5. The accident taught the reckless driver an important lesson.

6. The committee gave Michael Jordan an award after the season.

7. We picked a map for the trip.

8. The message from the ship was urgent.

9. Mother filled the jar with pennies, nickels, and dimes.

10. The cook added extra vegetables to the soup.

WORKSHEET 27

- Identify all parts of speech learned so far.
- Draw arrows from adjectives and adverbs to the words they modify.
- Write *O.P.* over the object of a preposition.
- Enclose prepositional phrases within parentheses.
- Label each prepositional phrase with either *ADJ.* or *ADV.*
- Draw arrows from prepositional phrases to the words they modify.
- Use Noun Function Cards 1–5:
    Put an *S.* over each subject.
    Circle each direct object.
    Put *P.N.* above each predicate nominative.

1. Mr. LaChance is a politician in Denver.

2. Mother is very happy with the new computer.

3. The cute dog is a female poodle.

4. Dad found the ball on the roof.

5. Thomas Jefferson was the third president of the United States.

6. Most caterpillars become butterflies.

7. She will be a speaker at the rally.

8. You fix the car, and I'll drive to town.

9. Roberta is a Democrat; I'm a Republican.

10. It was cold and rainy during the vacation.

WORKSHEET 28

- Identify all parts of speech learned so far.
- If a pronoun has been omitted, write it in and enclose it within parentheses.
- Draw arrows from adjectives and adverbs to the words they modify.
- Write O.P. over the object of a preposition.
- Enclose prepositional phrases within parentheses.
- Label each prepositional phrase with either ADJ. or ADV.
- Draw arrows from prepositional phrases to the words they modify.
- Use Noun Function Cards 1–5:
    Put an S. over each subject.
    Circle each direct object.
    Put P.N. above each predicate nominative.

1. Diamonds and rubies are valuable gems.

2. Geese fly from Canada to the southern United States during the fall.

3. She told me a good story.

4. Fire came from the engine near the tip of the wing.

5. I was shocked by the news from Washington.

6. We had orange juice and cereal for breakfast.

7. He'll be a nurse, and she'll be a doctor.

8. He tells funny jokes, and people laugh with him.

9. Pardon me.

10. Are you the woman from the insurance company?

QUIZ 4

(to be taken after completing Worksheet 28)

- Identify all parts of speech learned so far.
- If a pronoun has been omitted, write it in and enclose it within parentheses.
- Draw arrows from adjectives and adverbs to the words they modify.
- Write *O.P.* over the object of a preposition.
- Enclose prepositional phrases within parentheses.
- Label each prepositional phrase with either *ADJ.* or *ADV.*
- Draw arrows from prepositional phrases to the words they modify.
- Use Noun Function Cards 1-5:
    - Put an *S.* over each subject.
    - Circle each direct object.
    - Put a box around each indirect object.
    - Put *P.N.* above each predicate nominative.

1. I'll give Stella the sweater after recess.

2. He and Trudy will be in Detroit for several weeks.

3. Pip is a famous character in a book by Charles Dickens.

4. Take Max and Sal to the movies with you.

5. The people in the photograph are father and daughter.

6. At the rehearsal, the director showed me the lines for Act I.

7. I gave Mr. Makioka a knife for the steak.

8. The farmer sold apples and corn to the travelers.

9. The path is more slippery at the top of the hill.

10. Could the young woman be a professional dancer?

Bonus

Alice's Adventures in Wonderland has become a very famous book for children and adults.

WORKSHEET 29

- Identify all parts of speech learned so far.
- If a pronoun has been omitted, write it in and enclose it within parentheses.
- Draw arrows from adjectives and adverbs to the words they modify.
- Write *O.P.* over the object of a preposition.
- Enclose prepositional phrases within parentheses.
- Label each prepositional phrase with either *ADJ.* or *ADV.*
- Draw arrows from prepositional phrases to the words they modify.
- Use Noun Function Cards 1–7:
    Put an *S.* over each subject.
    Circle each direct object.
    Put *P.N.* above each predicate nominative.
    Write *N.D.A.* over nouns of direct address.

1. Will you come with us to the airport, Phillip?

2. A famous actor appears in the film.

3. Eva, have you finished the math yet?

4. Collect the trash in the backyard, Joe.

5. Mack Burton mowed the soccer field.

6. Help Roger with the luggage, David.

7. Cats and dogs are popular house pets.

8. You can't become a good tennis player without practice.

9. Alberta, are you a Girl Scout?

10. We went on a diet after the holidays.

WORKSHEET 30

- Identify all parts of speech learned so far.
- Write in any pronouns that have been omitted and enclose them in parentheses.
- Draw arrows from adjectives and adverbs to the words they modify.
- Write *O.P.* over the object of a preposition.
- Enclose prepositional phrases within parentheses.
- Label each prepositional phrase with either *ADJ.* or *ADV.*
- Draw arrows from prepositional phrases to the words they modify.
- Use Noun Function Cards 1–8:
    Put an *S.* over each subject.
    Circle each direct object.
    Put *P.N.* above each predicate nominative.
    Write *N.D.A.* over nouns of direct address.
    Write *APP.* above each appositive.

1. The friendly mailman, Mr. Bettencourt, retired yesterday.

2. The only store in town will close soon.

3. The television show, *Sesame Street*, is popular with many young children.

4. Queen Victoria was a powerful ruler.

5. Katarina Kline, the chairperson, ended the meeting promptly.

6. The Tin Man is a character in *The Wizard of Oz*.

7. Buck became sheriff of the county.

8. Be kind to animals.

9. Louisa May Alcott is the author of the book.

10. Turn the corner, but be careful, Pat.

Posttest

Write your answers to the following questions on the lines at the right.

Sentence 1

The large bull charged angrily across the field.

1. Name the adjective. _____ 1.
2. Name the adverb. _____ 2.
3. Name the preposition. _____ 3.
4. Name the subject. _____ 4.
5. Name the object of the preposition. _____ 5.
6. What word does *angrily* modify? _____ 6.

Sentence 2

I sent Hal a long letter today.

7. Name the direct object. _____ 7.
8. Name the adverb. _____ 8.
9. Name the verb. _____ 9.
10. Name the pronoun. _____ 10.
11. Name the article. _____ 11.
12. Name the indirect object. _____ 12.
13. What word does *long* modify? _____ 13.

Copyright © 1992, 1982
Permission is granted to reproduce this test for use with *The Winston Grammar Program.*

Sentence 3

Do not drink the soda before lunch, Nancy.

14. How many nouns are there in Sentence 3? _____ 14.
15. Name the direct object. _____ 15.
16. Name the noun of direct address. _____ 16.
17. Name the subject. _____ 17.
18. Name the verb phrase. _____ 18.
19. Name the adverb. _____ 19.

Sentence 4

We are afraid of the snake, and I wish it would disappear.

20. Name the coordinating conjunction. _____ 20.
21. Name the helping verb. _____ 21.
22. Name the "being" or "linking" verb. _____ 22.
23. How many subjects are there in Sentence 4? _____ 23.
24. Name the adjective. _____ 24.

Sentence 5

Wow, the story is really scary!

25. Name the verb. _____ 25.
26. Name the adverb. _____ 26.
27. Name the interjection. _____ 27.
28. Name the article. _____ 28.

Sentence 6

She and Lorenzo were the best actors in the school play.

29. How many adjectives are there in Sentence 6? _____ 29.
30. Name the object of the preposition. _____ 30.
31. Name the subject(s). _____ 31.
32. Name the predicate nominative. _____ 32.
33. What part of speech is *school*? _____ 33.